Grapevines

Tameron Colbert

BookLeaf
Publishing

India | USA | UK

Presentation by *BookLeaf Publishing*

Web: www.bookleafpub.com

E-mail: info@bookleafpub.com

ISBN: 9789360940089

First edition 2024

To my readers,

Thank you for choosing to give the book a chance. I am really humbled and very appreciative that you have taken the time to read and take a chance on my words. Every poem in this book is based on the old saying "I heard it through the Grapevine"; Each poem has been a stepping stone in my past and my present. Whenever you read these poems, each has its unique theme and they all are a part of me in some way. Some poems tell stories, some of them talk about my inner demons, and some are just purely expressions of what I am currently dealing with in my life. I know as people we all have our experiences, our own set of suffering, and our own set of joys that have shaped us into who we are and who we want to be.

-Tameron Colbert

Cherokee Rose

Back street roads,
Where are you taking me?

Passing through the broken street lights,
Just like my memories,
Those are moments I can never get back.

Through, the southern fields,
The tears of my past fall next,
To my self-hatred.

For a moment, I smile seeing where I have come
from,
For a moment, I feel happiness,
Although, I have contemplated along the trail of
tears.
While seeking forgiveness, for my past, my
present, and my future.

The sun shines on the broken glass,
A refraction of time that is mended on southern
nights,
Though my feet have cuts and a blood trail,
My tears comfort me to push forward.

Night comes calling,
As I continue to spiral,
Echoing down the road,
As the abyss swallows me,
My knees tremble and my heart gives in.

My eyes close embracing the darkness,
As the back roads, speak to me
Ominous, bleak, and loving,
Are the voices I hear,
I look down at my palm,
There sits the rose.

The petals glow vividly,
Vibrating in my palm,
It tells me to close my eyes,
And embrace its song.

Home

Everything feels the same, but doesn't look the same,
Yet, the sun also rises on the broken home and bitter bones.

The airport feels ominous and cultural,
My heart speaks to me in a language I can't understand,
But longs for a hug.

All the familiar faces still look the same,
But my mask is too broken to hide behind my crooked smile.

I feel the love of my family,
The warm hugs from my gentle mother,
The sharpness of my sister,

The wisdom of my father,
And the humor of my cousin.

On my shoulders
I feel the emptiness of survivor's guilt,
And the more I shake it away,
The more it feeds on me each day.

Everything doesn't feel the same, nor does it
look the same,
Yet, the moon shines on my past, as the night
swallows me.

I visited my grandmother for the first time in a
year,
She sits lakeside, tombstone after tombstone,
Feeling a cold, concrete, shiver string on my
spine.

Memories drift past me,
As I find myself half awake and half asleep,
My friends have found their own,
My family smiles through the broken bones

While I try to figure out if I deserve to come
home.

Breezin' With The Shadows

Juke jams and silent lambs,
The black boy runs
Sweating, dying, and singing.

Speak to him,
As the roots and vines spiral the whips on his
back,
His soul blows a spiritual
While staring eye to eye
With the cloak, stalking from the shadows.

The dirt from his nails
"Why ya skin dirty?",
The curl from his wail,

"Momma why it hurt so much?"
Feeds the pavement of devastation,
As the shadows dance to a jazz tune
Around him.

"To be you must be close to despair,
You must remain a shadow in,
In our skin-head society."
Speak to them,
Sing it in a way only dem negros will understand
"Here boy, take dis here cotton flower,
Dis is ya place on the world."

Juke Jams and Silent Lambs
A little black girl cries with a flower,
In a field surrounded by piercing suns and silent
petals,
Don't cry, your tears must turn into a song.

Coltrane tunes in the breezy afternoon,
Dries her tears blazing a monsoon
May the cotton wash their sins away
Because tears do fade away,
But the scars on their skin
Will forever dance in the fields.

Museum

Through the neon lights,
In Passing Under the Stars,
There is a blur in my eyes
That keeps making me fall apart.

Here we are staring eye to eye,
Pain for Pain,
Peeling back the gallery
As the night shines,
The refraction displays a reflection of us.

Take my hand for the first time,
As I watch you drown,
In the slithering of your arteries clouded,
Your gentle hand evaporates from me.

Where did we go wrong?
Phasing in and out of our world,
Tears acidic to the pavement,
Steam slowly becoming our paradox,

The stars laugh at us,
As you take my hand,
Let us evaporate together,
As the wind of our souls vaporizes your
thoughts.

Melt into my arms
under this streetlight
Dancing our love
Into the muses of the night.

A Lily For a Sista in September

Stretch in the morning dew,
Open your heart to absorb the views
Of the sounds of a daunting train

She sees the madness,
Hoping to save what's left of her
Crying in the night sky,
Hoping we speak back.

"Why must I suffer alone?"
Contemplating, the cycles
That curl the sweat in her hair,
As the tears fall from the bricks in her heart.

On the escape,

She heard the screams
The sirens, and the children laughing,
Wondering why the stars are so far from her
Her mind chains as the fires rise from the streets,

In that moment,
Her mother wails and her father hits,
Until she finds a butterfly soaring through
The stirring mist.

The Songs in the Sea of Mirrors

My feet are bare, As I head toward the sea
The dance between loneliness and madness
Are the only things guiding me,
The sands disappear, as the glass begins to cut
deep,
Songs and melodies cry out all around me.

The sea of mirrors reflects as it draws me in for
a kiss
I close my eyes hoping this will end,
Until the cracking of the mirrors
Tells me to gently open my eyes.

There in the middle of the sea,
Mirrors are all around me,
I look down to see my heart,
Beating in my hand,
I am frozen as I watch all the mirrors:

To my left,
A woman rocking herself in solitude,
Crying at the loss of her son,
Her husband runs and quilts her with passion.

To my right,
A man playing Russian roulette,
After losing his family,
In his arms,
His brothers, rush in and embrace his pain.

Below me,
A little girl searches for her brother,
Who was murdered in front of her.
Her parents, in pain, shower her with love
To mend those memories.

Above me,
A room, showered with flowers,
Feeding the ambiance,
Smiles of a family, that is broken,
Waiting as a queen,
Prepares to give birth.

My heart, My soul, My love,
The muses among us begin to rise from the sea,
Laughing and chanting we are family.

Vines

One night,
In love, we pass
In blush, we ascend,
One day we must taste
The fruit, the maple
Flowers of the body
Searching for the flaming rose,
the souls dance along the wet bough,
stringing the violin of the heart.

Matrix

All things can't last,
But the future is only with you.
Some worlds could be two
If the game is just a game,
Until you see that
We are just becoming strange
To a materialistic fantasy
As we decline the possibility
Only to fathom, that dreaming
Is our only reality.

Albatross

As I pictured you sailing,
Across the seas to Heaven Gate,
Stretching your arms out to me
As your eyes are watching God.

I hear the hymns, the angels,
All the praises, as the serene view
In my heart cries for you to come back
I still can hear you say "Hey Nana Baby,"
As your eyes were watching God.

My right hand still burns bright red from,
You always pick me up when I fall,
From the way you taught me to love,
Always be faithful, and always
Trust in the flowers Christ always gives,
As your eyes were watching God.

Your love and divinity departed the Red Sea,
My eternal rose, I watch you from earth
Hoping to look up and see you free from your
pain,
Wishing I could have been there by your side,
Just want to have you cheer me on one more
time
Now you must sail and be free as the rose petals
Fall from the sky
As your eyes cried with God.

May the angels be with you,
May serenity guide you,
As I wish to give you my words one last time,
As I watch the Albatross fly across the sky,
Feeling the wind and closing my eyes
While the tears of joy tumble down my face,
I feel your hand gently touch my hand,
As you say, "I love you Puny"
I fall into your arms crying
As our eyes watch God together.

Eclipse Of Hearts

Love,
A Horizon compelled between
Two Suns and a Moon
Dance carefully,

We depict such a beautiful Horizon
Of compelled colors of blues, purples, and
yellows
To form the perfect love for the sun itself

Have you felt the sun?
Brighten, to make the perfect day
Seem infinite...
And turn the tide of beauty
That enriches the inequities of your life.

Have you ever been sold into trickery?
That loving the sun and putting it
On your shoulders, could forever
Put an Eclipse over your
Heart.

For The First Time

She sits at the front door, staring at the sky
Her eyes are lit with the dim of the sun,
A tear creaks down towards her nose,
Not knowing where to go like sheep in a field,
The day darkens, and as she sits, the streetlights
Begin to illuminate the crevices of her face.

A broken vase sits near the entrance of the door,
Dead flowers have no weight as,
Her eyes are full with the night,
As she tears the house apart, searching for
answers
"Tell me what's wrong."
She breathes fire from the entrance of the door.

The rain kisses the pavement like
Distant lovers meeting for the first time,
The street light flickers,
As the night begins to commune with her,
The tears scorch in the light,
As he finds her, falling into quicksand,
He takes her hand, and pulls her up softly,
"No one can see my tears in the rain," she says.

Their hearts beat to the rhythm of the rain,
As it dances on their face,
He reaches into the depths of his soul,
And pulls out a flower and places it on the left
side
Of her hair,
Brushing away all the existence of time.

Down the crescent side of his face,
His tears and the rain become one
Where he tells her,
"All I see is you."

The rain freezes, the street light bends
On the reflection of their odyssey,
Where flowers bloom,
Watching the tears fall to her lips.

Shady Grove 5:30

The hourglass begins to tip over,
Everyone walks around with mud on their faces
Until he walks through concrete,
A scent challenges his heart
Softly like the harp,
His feet turn into stone.

The sand rushes from the hourglass
Like ants from a mound,
She is warm with eyes like caramel in the sun,
The dim lights, begin to break all existence one
by one,
As her intuition plays a tune.

The station seems smaller
As they turn to each other,
Their eyes are filled with flames,
Like a phoenix kissing the sun,
She walks in magnetism, as the station
disappears

He walks in skepticism, filling his hands with
flowers
Glowing in the darkness,
She calls out to him, as her voice echoes like a
scream from a mountain,
He reaches out, as the flowers light her eyes,
The words are muted, as the station-like time
forever keeps moving,

She disappears into the sea of men,
Where he dives unconditionally, searching for
her soul,
Until, the hourglass breaks, and the sand floods
his mind, and
She embraces him, where the moon meets the
stars
Reflecting on the day she met him, as he dies in
her arms.

Green Line 6:36

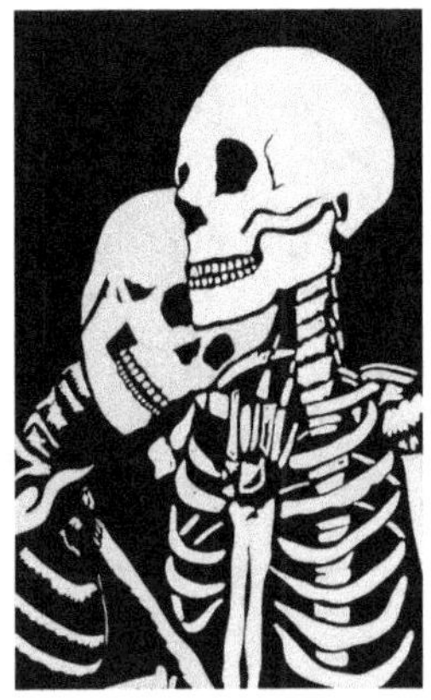

While walking,
The world never seemed more clear
The air is filled with ash
While I sit on the train wondering helplessly into
fear
There I notice, the swaying eyes flooding the
train
On such an empty night

Two lovers,
Both carrying the sun in the weight of smiles
He touches her face, in the veil of the night,
The train bumps and sings
She falls into his arms and laughs
Watching as the lights disappear in the tunnel

The lemon crush of the lovers
Continues as I journal,
Her laugh fills the lights on the train,
His touch scorches the night of flames,
For the moment, their eyes filled with the stars.

Time, irrelevant, to the muse passing them
The world feels empty,
He tip-toes his way, toward the light on her lips,
While the noise in her head cries longing for
him,
The light and darkness in the tunnels splash on
their faces.

The petals begin to fall,
As she begins to cry, dancing with emotion,
He gently, brushes her hair, from the glow of her
face,
There is a gentle whisper between the two,
As the magnetism between folds the metal of the
train
I am left to wonder if they ever kissed in that
rain.

Autumn Of Snow

Mornings in the drapes of the failing sun,
The grey skies are melancholy,
Hearing the groans in your sleep,
As we dance around in the sheets,
Roaming the roses of ideas,
Feeling the warmth of your coconut kisses.

We star-gazed for an hour when the sun began to
bloom,
Your gentle hand was so cold,
Of a depressing heart,
Sing to me, that one song over and over again,
Let us make love to our bagels and be one like
birds.

Through the damp light-hearted kitchen
The explosion in the horizon of your gestures,
Turn us to the hardened window,
As we slide, into the cool ignorance of the air
The Promethean of your heart manages to glare.

One step at a time,

As I gently grab your hand,
Feeling the fire of intertwined lines,
We expose our southern nights, and
Change them into Snow.

We pause,
Deeper than the statues of U-St,
Slowly, holy, fullness of life in our grasp,
Gently, the coldness of your breath fills my
lungs with glee,
The song of the birds melts our trees,

Here we are,
Saxophones in the distance,
Filling our time over time,
In a sentimental mood.

In that moment,
Time has given me a gift,
The Autumn in your eyes,
And the first taste of your lips.

Elysium

In the isles of our bed
Her eyes closed, without words,
Filling all the voids that moaned within,
In my arms, I felt her eyes drift into the veil.

The days turn to years, and time is faced with
broken clocks
I watch her dance along the flowers, grappling
with the depths
Of her humanity,
The sensuality that breaks when death soothes
your inhumanity.

Tears poison the flowers,
As I stare violently into the night,
Death holds out her hand, to gently touch my
face,

Harden, cold, lights and nebulas fill my heart
Death catches me,
While I float past Elysium wondering about the
waters at night.

The lost souls, all kiss me passionately on the
lips,
As I am pulled into a well of endless nights,
There she waits for me,
My muse singing our song only I could hear,
Death plays the lyre, giving me a chance to live,

Across the golden field,
She sings to me as I run to her,
The tears the fold of our reality,
We embrace each other, as we set fire to rain,
Our tears, invigorate the blooming of existence,
As we kiss,
Death stops us as it takes each of our hands,
While we all pause,
To watch the sunset.

Thoughts in November

On this night of illumination,
The flowers became the stars of the earth
The trees drift in and out of shades.

They pass along with winter's breath,
Tasting the feeling of being deserialized,
Running through the corridors of my mind,
A memory falls and shatters into the earth.

The chamber hearts,
Search for faded pieces,
Alone on the deserted road.

The lights melt into the pavement
Breaking the molds of our reality,
There is a pause and whispers in the distance.

Their eyes and souls,
Are frozen as one,
I search through the wounds and needles,

A soft touch on my face,
Branding me, as she turns and walks away.

Jazz Into The Sunset

Let me illuminate you,
Into the sunset where the reds blend with the
orange,
As I but not I flow into the gallows
Pass the severed stairs
As one loves timeless flares
While one dares,
To sprinkle pass the fruitless shares
Granting vulgarity among the many hairs
Time, how time is only meant to stare
Laughing at us as chains begin to bear
Can we go,
Petal by Petal upon a dare
Grazing vines, while soulless to share
Let us jazz,
Our distance into the vail horizon
As we rise together as the spring on Orion
boundless souled in iron.
Here we are,
Where time disintegrates and smile
Where we lay and grow pale
Time watches us as we become frail
While there it sets upon destination
As we appall our only devastation
As you hold your head low,

My sax plays something for you
In the drowsiness, you feel without navigation
But we are here,
As I forward my steps, time begins to ache
While here you glow distant from my pain
Until you are forever lost in the depths of my
flame.

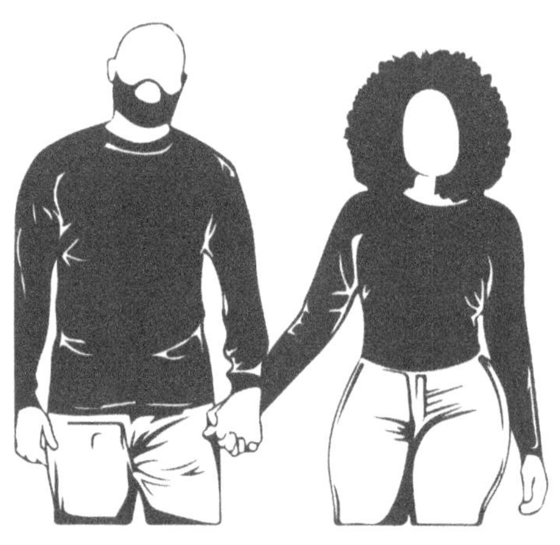

Fear

My dream is gone now,
As my heart does not know why,
I suffocate there.

Lament

Cut your chest open,
Let your heart bleed out into,
The soft white cloud here.

The Songs Of Gaza

A child sits in a disintegrating building
Singing and staring out into the night,
Her face is charred with ash and blood
As the tears roll down her eyes,
Her wounds begin to open.

Through the sirens and explosions
A man flashes through the crowd,
Pushing, shoving, and panicking, to reach his
family.
   Through the sand, he sees his wife and child,
   Calling out to him, as he runs with the blood
on his sandals,
The building comes towering down.

                  The flares illuminate the
void in the sky,
                  As the people cling to
the pots and pans,
                    For scraps of food,
                  Dust fills their lungs,
from the dryness of water
                    As the violence
dances on,

                          So do the tears of
mothers.
A group of elderly women and men
Begin to pray,
As they watch a ditch,
  Cemented with blue body bags
      Sink silently into the Earth.

        A medic holds a newborn in his arms,
        Bathed in dust, barely clinging to life,
            While under the rubble, a little boy,
        Gasps for air, watching the sun fade away.

                A family stands around white
sheets,
                Soaked in blood,
            A father and son fall to their
knees,
                A mother clinches her
children tighter
                    As their aunt begins to cry.

      For the greater good,
      Why must we endure evil?
      Thousands, walk among tombstones,
              As a child and their sibling
              Dance with war
      And the night flashes on.

Calling out for their mother
Whose body is unknown.

Among the destruction
    A woman plays the violin,
        A song is heard in the distance
    As a father shelters his family,
    A child who is living for another child,
        Smiles another day.

When can we finally,
    Find a paradox in this life,
    Where war does not take,
        All we have, All we love
    And turn it into peace.

Hope

The Boy and girl play
Together in the schoolyard,
As a casket rolls.

As I lay Dying

As I lay dying,
On a bed of thorns,
Searching for the stars,
That has walked the earth.

In a grave,
On the summer's eve,
The soil bathes, as I
Search for filaments through life.

The crisp cries, of dried screams,
Are echoed through, a field of The Walking
Dead,
As I, six feet beneath the earth,
Make friends with earthworms,
And lay still on the eve, where summers
Come to an end.

Years pass,
As the echoes are silent,
Tears, rain, and pleas water the grass.

I wonder, why I can't open my eyes,
To understand, why dying comes easier
Than living.

The sun sets over the cemetery,
As shadows kiss the tombstones,
All the voices,
Wail to the falling sun, as they march
Over us.

Nina Mosley

Coconut and honey scents on your turtle neck,
Tell me, do you think I just want sex,
or do I want you in my wet dreams?
Hate me if you will, but I can't deny your
African Diaspora.

 See, I wish that was the case,
That dying, divine elegance, of your laughter
Alters my perception,
And even disintegrates time.

I want to compare you to a painting, the sea,
Nature, fruits, and every image possible,
You are just that kind of woman.
I feel the roots in your hair,
The motivation of your passion,

And the sweat of your barriers.

  Bare with me, because sex
    Is a short-term reward,
      But your love,
Is like holding a butterfly for the first time,
    Gentle, soft, and full of possibilities.

        I'm not the brotha to the night,
          Because night just passes, and then
          We go our separate ways.
      I want you in places in my heart,
          Only I want you to know exists.

Smother me, with your knowledge,
Your struggle, your tears, your fears of the
future.
Let us take down our barriers,
And drift endlessly in love,
Where there is no such thing as time.

        I can't let you just walk out of my life,
              Watching your curls fade,
          Knowing you can love someone else,
          Knowing that I can't protect you,
          Knowing that I will run after a train for
you,
            Even if it never stops.

Even here and now,
If I never get to see you again,
Embrace your touch, laugh with you, cry with
you,
I will, above this plane, of false living,
I will come find you, in the afterlife
So that I can give you flowers
For all eternity.

Suicide Note

If I were to let,
The luminous, calm, eyes of the ocean erode me
away,
No one would ever know.

9 789360 940089